AFRICAN GREY PARROTS AS PETS

Everything You Need To Know About African Grey Parrots Ownership Including Housing, Health Care, Sickness Signs, Training, Conversation And Why They Make Excellent Pets.

BY

RAPH FRANCIS

COPYRIGHT © 2024 ALL RIGHT RESERVED

TABLE OF CONTENTS

CHAPTER 1:
INTRODUCING AFRICAN GREY PARROTS

CHAPTER 2:
WHY GET A PET AFRICAN GREY?

CHAPTER 3:
GETTING READY FOR YOUR AFRICAN GREY PARROT

CHAPTER 4:
COMPREHENDING AFRICAN GREY PARROT BEHAVIOR

CHAPTER 5:
FURNISHING YOUR AFRICAN GREY PARROT WITH THE PERFECT ENVIRONMENT

CHAPTER 6:
RECOGNIZING AND FULFILLING THE NUTRITIONAL REQUIREMENTS OF YOUR AFRICAN GREY

CHAPTER 7:
GIVING YOUR AFRICAN GREY EXERCISE, PLAY, AND ENRICHMENT

CHAPTER 8:
GETTING TO KNOW YOUR AFRICAN GREY AND FORMING BONDS

CHAPTER 9:
AFRICAN GREY PARROT HEALTH AND COMMON ILLNESSES

CHAPTER 10:
AFRICAN GREY PARROT TRAINING

CHAPTER 11:
AFRICAN GREY PARROT ENRICHMENT AND ACTIVITIES

CHAPTER 12:
COMPREHENDING AFRICAN GREY COMMUNICATION AND BEHAVIOR

CHAPTER 13:
FREQUENTLY ASKED QUESTION AND ANSWERS (FAQS)

CHAPTER 1:

INTRODUCING AFRICAN GREY PARROTS

Many people consider African Grey Parrots to be among the most captivating and intelligent kinds of birds. Bird lovers and pet owners worldwide have fallen in love with these parrots because of their remarkable cognitive powers and amazing ability to imitate human speech. An introduction to the interesting world of African Grey Parrots is given in this chapter, which also covers the species, origins, history, and distinctions between the two main varieties of African Greys, the Timneh African Grey and the Congo African Grey.

A Synopsis of the Species

The medium-sized African Grey Parrot, or Psittacus erithacus, is a resident of the rainforests of Central and West Africa. They are distinguished by their mostly grey feathers, which contrast sharply with their pale face and bright red tail. Although not as flashy as other kinds of parrots with vivid colors, they have a sleek, sophisticated appearance that contributes to their allure.

African Grey Parrots normally have a length of 12 to 14 inches and a wingspan of 18 to 20 inches. They are a particularly big species of parrot, weighing between 400 and 600 grams. They are very intelligent and strong, which enables them to utilize their feet and beak in incredibly creative ways. Because of their intellect, they do, however, need a great deal of mental contact and stimulation, which may provide owners with both opportunities and challenges.

The remarkable capacity of African Grey Parrots to imitate sounds, including human speech, is one of their most well-known characteristics. They are regarded as among the most talkative parrots, able to acquire large vocabulary and often use words contextually. But their vocal prowess is just one facet of their nuanced personalities. When given the necessary care and attention, these very observant and sensitive birds create strong emotional relationships with their owners, which makes them wonderful companions.

Origin and History

Both in the natural and in human civilization, the African Grey Parrot has a long and fascinating history. They are indigenous to the thick rainforests of Angola, Cameroon, Congo, Ivory Coast, Ghana, and Uganda. There, they dwell in great flocks and use a variety of vocalizations to interact with one another. They obtain all the fruit, nuts, and lush greenery they need to survive in their native environment.

Humans and African Grey Parrots have a long history together, dating back thousands of years. African Grey Parrots are said to have been domesticated by the Egyptians, and historical accounts indicate that the Romans and Greeks also held them in high regard. In many communities, their social character and capacity for speech imitation made them a prestige and luxury symbol. African Greys were introduced to Europe by European explorers and merchants in the fifteenth century, solidifying their status as exotic and perceptive pets.

African Grey Parrots have gained popularity in the pet sector over the last several decades, which has increased knowledge about their requirements and habits. But growing popularity has also made conservation more difficult, since illicit poaching and habitat destruction threaten wild populations. In order to ensure that these amazing birds may survive and prosper in their native habitat, several groups now strive to safeguard African Grey Parrots in the wild.

African Grey Parrot Types: Timneh vs. Congo

Although they are sometimes referred to as a single species, African Grey Parrots are really divided into two subspecies: Psittacus erithacus erithacus, which is found in Congo, and Psittacus erithacus timneh, which is found in Timneh. While there are numerous similarities between these two subspecies, there are also some significant distinctions that may affect a potential owner's decision.

African Grey Parrot of the Congo

With an average length of 13 to 14 inches, the Congo African Grey is the bigger of the two subspecies. Its brilliant red tail feathers, which contrast dramatically with the rest of its plumage, are its most distinguishing trait. Its feathers are a lighter, silvery-grey tint. The more central parts of Africa, which include the Congo, Gabon, and Cameroon, are home to Congo African Greys.

Congo African Greys are renowned for their keen intellect and remarkable vocal range. They pick things up quickly and can comprehend words and sentences in context. Many Congo Greys show extreme devotion and dedication to their human partners, forming close ties with them. They may be sensitive, however, and in order to flourish, they need a steady, stimulating environment.

Timneh Grey Parrot, African

The Timneh African Grey's plumage has a richer charcoal-grey tone and is darker than other African Greys. Its length typically ranges from 11 to 13 inches. The Timneh Grey's tail is a deeper shade of maroon than the Congo Grey's vivid red tail. In addition, the Timneh's beak has a blend of black and pale horn color, which gives it a somewhat distinct look from the Congo Grey's full black beak.

Timneh Greys are indigenous to western Africa, which includes nations like Sierra Leone and Liberia. When it comes to personality, Timneh Greys are sometimes characterized as being less prone to worry and more autonomous than their Congolese counterparts. They could need less care and consolation since they are usually better competent to adjust to new situations. They still need mental stimulation, however, since they are quite bright and need to prevent boredom and destructive behavior.

Perceptual and Emotional Intelligence

Many people agree that African Grey Parrots are among the most intellectual non-human animals. According to studies, they have cognitive capacities similar to those of young toddlers, including the capacity to comprehend cause and effect, solve complicated puzzles, and even display some emotional intelligence.

Working with Dr. Irene Pepperberg, one of the most well-known African Grey Parrots, Alex, showed amazing comprehension of color, form, number, and even emotions. Alex's research has shed light on parrots' cognitive abilities by demonstrating that they use words meaningfully and are not just copying them.

But this intellect has a profound emotional side to it. It is well known that African Grey Parrots are very perceptive to both their surroundings and the feelings of the people who live with them. They are sociable beings that become worried, nervous, or even sad when left alone for extended periods of time. Because of this, potential owners need to be ready to devote a lot of time and energy to satisfying their parrot's emotional requirements.

To sum up, African Grey Parrots are amazing birds with distinct personalities and amazing skills. They need a committed and experienced owner who can provide them the right attention, mental stimulation, and company. In the next chapters, as we get further into the intricacies of owning African Greys, we'll look at how to provide an atmosphere that is stimulating and conducive to these amazing birds' success.

CHAPTER 2:

WHY GET A PET AFRICAN GREY?

Often referred to as the "Einsteins of the bird world," African Grey Parrots are an intriguing option for pet owners. They are highly prized because to their reputation for intellect, emotional complexity, and amazing speech mimicking. But choosing to own an African Grey requires careful consideration because of their intricate demands, which call for a lot of time, attention, and understanding. We will discuss the benefits of owning an African Grey as a pet, possible drawbacks, and what makes them such special friends in this chapter.

Personality Characteristics and IQ

Celebrated for having remarkable intellect, frequently likened to a toddler's in humans, African Greys are very intelligent animals. These parrots may be trained to imitate a broad range of noises, such as phones, doorbells, and even the voices of other family members, in addition to human speech. Their comprehension of word context is very impressive. For instance, many African Grey owners believe that their birds can pronounce certain words when it's appropriate, such "hello" when they enter a room or "goodbye" when they depart. They differ from other bird species due to their sophisticated cognitive abilities, which also adds a degree of interaction that many bird fans find alluring.

An African Grey's intellect extends beyond imitation. These birds know how to solve problems. They can figure out how to unlock cage doors, use their feet and beaks to handle items, and even play memory- and strategy-based games. For owners, this mental acuity is both an advantage and a difficulty. On the one hand, this indicates that they are interesting pets that are always willing to learn new things. However, because of their intellect, they need ongoing enrichment and excitement to avoid boredom, which may result in negative behaviors.

African Greys possess both emotional intelligence and emotional sensitivity. They are gregarious birds that develop close relationships with their owners. This relationship may be quite fulfilling since these birds often become devoted, loving friends. If their social needs are not addressed, it also implies that they are more vulnerable to emotional problems including stress, worry, and depression. They are very susceptible to changes in their surroundings or daily schedule, which may sometimes lead to undesirable behaviors like excessive vocalizations or plucking of feathers. Because of this, owners of African Greys need to be ready to provide their pets a regular daily schedule and a secure, caring atmosphere.

Benefits and Drawbacks of Keeping an African Grey

Consider the benefits and drawbacks of having such a sophisticated and demanding pet before choosing to adopt an African Grey. Here are some important things to think about:

The first benefit is intellect and trainability. Among the easiest parrots to teach are African Greys. They may pick up instructions, tricks, and even how to express their demands if they are given enough time and attention. Because of their intelligence, they are quite engaging, which many owners find to be very satisfying.

2. *Speech and Mimicry:* African Greys are unmatched in their capacity to imitate human speech. Through their vocalizations, they often develop distinctive personalities and are able to acquire huge vocabularies. For the owners, this may provide them with a lifetime of delight and enjoyment.

3. *Emotional Bond:* African Greys and their human caretakers develop enduring relationships. They make devoted and caring pets because of their amiable disposition and need for company. They provide solace and a sense of emotional connection since they are able to sense their owners' feelings.

4. *Longevity:* African Grey Parrots make enduring friends since they may live for 40 to 60 years when given the right care. This lifespan is a benefit for people looking for lifelong companionship since it enables owners to build strong, enduring bonds with their birds.

Cons: 1. High Maintenance: One of the most demanding parrot species is the African Grey, which is also characterized by its intelligence. To keep them from becoming bored and developing behavioral issues, they need social contact and ongoing mental stimulation. This entails spending a few hours a day engaging in play, training, and enrichment activities with your bird.

2. Emotional Sensitivity: It's well known that African Greys have high emotional sensitivity. If they experience stress or neglect, they may experience anxiety or sadness and turn to destructive activities like plucking feathers. Owners need to be ready to provide a steady, stimulating atmosphere as well as emotional support.

3. Noise Levels: African Greys may be quite talkative even if their volume is not as high as that of certain other parrot species. They imitate sounds and even begin to imitate noises from the home, such as appliances or alarms. While this may be charming, it may also be annoying in a peaceful apartment building or home.

4. Long-Term Commitment: Owning an African Grey requires a significant, long-term commitment because of their extended lifetime. Given their 60-year lifespan, these parrots have the potential to outlast their owners. Prospective owners should think about the bird's long-term care, particularly what would happen to it if they are unable to provide for it.

Realizing the Assignation

Choosing to live with an African Grey Parrot is a lifestyle decision, not simply a pastime. You should never let these birds alone for extended periods of time as pets. They will develop strong emotional bonds with their owners and have a strong need for interaction. When these requirements are ignored, major emotional and behavioral issues may result. It is crucial, then, to assess your daily routine, your capacity for regular care, and your desire to invest time in your bird.

Time is one of the most important factors for prospective African Grey owners. For these parrots to be happy and healthy, they need constant engagement and attention—often for many hours each day. African Greys may not be the ideal companion for someone who has a hectic lifestyle or takes numerous trips. Lack of excitement and loneliness may swiftly result in harmful habits that are hard to stop once they begin.

The financial commitment is another important one. African Grey Parrots need premium food, toys, and routine veterinary examinations, along with specialist avian care. These birds are known to be destructive, particularly when bored, thus toys that stimulate the mind are essential and should be changed often. Prospective owners should also be informed that African Greys need a large cage as well as daily exercise and exploring time outdoors.

Finally, since African Grey Parrots live a long life, owning one is a lifetime commitment. These birds have a lifespan of many decades, unlike many other pets. Owners need to make arrangements for their parrot's long-term care, including what will happen if circumstances or health prevent them from being able to provide for the bird.

African Grey: Why Select One?

Many bird fans find owning African Greys to be very fulfilling pets, despite their limitations. They are special companions because of their intellect, charisma, and capacity for bonding with their owners. The bond that forms between those who are prepared to put in the time and energy needed to care for an African Grey may be very satisfying.

An person who appreciates giving their African Grey pet mental and emotional stimulation and values interaction with their pet is the perfect owner. These birds may provide steady company and are best suited for people or families that spend the most of the day at home. With the correct care and upbringing, an African Grey Parrot may grow to be a cherished family member who offers lifelong friendships and entertainment.

To sum up, African Grey Parrots are wonderful pets for anyone who are ready to attend to their intricate requirements. They are interesting and fascinating company because of their intellect, loving disposition, and speaking skills. However, because of their long-term commitment, emotional sensitivity, and need for stimulation, potential owners should carefully evaluate if they are prepared for the obligations that come with keeping such an exceptional bird.

CHAPTER 3:

GETTING READY FOR YOUR AFRICAN GREY PARROT

Although it calls for careful planning, bringing an African Grey Parrot into your household can be an exciting and gratifying experience. To guarantee the wellbeing of these very sensitive and clever birds, their special demands must be satisfied. We'll go over how to get your house and way of life ready for your new feathery friend in this chapter. This chapter will walk you through all the important aspects of getting ready for your African Grey Parrot, from picking the ideal cage and creating the ideal habitat to assembling the required materials and comprehending your bird's psychological requirements.

Designing the Ideal Living Area

Making a cozy, secure, and engaging living environment for an African Grey Parrot is one of the most important parts of being ready for one. An African Grey need plenty of space to go about, investigate, and exercise since it is a very clever and energetic bird. A well-designed habitat is important for the bird's physical and emotional well-being in addition to being comfortable.

Design and Size of Cages

Your African Grey Parrot's cage will serve as its permanent home, so it's important to choose one that is both roomy and safe. Being medium-sized to big parrots, African Greys need a cage with plenty of room to play, climb, and extend their wings. Larger is always preferable, but a decent cage should be at least 36 inches long, 24 inches wide, and 48 inches tall. Horizontal bars are also necessary in the cage since African Greys love to climb and will utilize them to navigate their space.

The bar spacing is another important consideration. To prevent the bird's head from being trapped, the distance between the bars should not be more than ¾ inch. Because African Greys are skilled escape artists and can readily pick how to open basic locks, the cage should also have a robust locking system.

To keep your bird's feet healthy and active, you'll need to offer many perches within the cage that vary in thickness and texture. Natural wood perches are the best since they promote climbing and provide your bird a cozy place to rest. Steer clear of consistent, smooth perches since they may eventually cause foot issues. You should also provide your African Grey with a range of toys, swings, and ladders to pique their natural interest and provide entertainment.

Setting and Position of the Cage

The location of the cage is as crucial as the cage itself. African Grey Parrots are gregarious birds who get great pleasure from interacting with people. Because of this, the cage has to be positioned in the middle of the house so the bird can see and participate in all of the everyday activities. Nonetheless, giving your bird a feeling of security is just as crucial. Keep the cage away from drafty spots, doors, and windows, since these might make the bird feel vulnerable or frightened by loud noises and abrupt movements.

African Greys also need a healthy mix of natural light and darkness for their mental and physical well-being. Natural sunshine exposure is necessary for the manufacture of Vitamin D, which maintains strong bones and feathers. If your residence receives little natural light, you may need to spend money on full-spectrum lighting intended for birds. On the other hand, African Greys need 10 to 12 hours of uninterrupted sleep every night in order to maintain their mental stability and overall health, therefore it's critical to provide them with a peaceful, dark sleeping area. You may help make sure your bird receives the rest it needs by covering the cage at night with a permeable cloth.

Play and Inclusion

Being among the smartest species of parrots, African Greys need continual mental stimulation to avoid boredom, which may result in destructive behavior, excessive vocalization, or feather plucking, among other behavioral issues. When getting ready for your African Grey, enrichment need to be your main focus. This entails offering a wide assortment of toys, puzzles, and foraging activities that test the bird's ability to solve problems and promote instinctive behaviors like chewing and shredding.

To keep your bird's cage interesting and engaging, turn the toys around often. Particularly helpful are toys that need the bird to pull or move elements in order to obtain goodies, such puzzle feeders or toys that stimulate object manipulation. Foraging toys are designed to simulate the natural habits of African Greys when they forage for food in the wild. They also provide African Greys mental and physical activity by hiding food or treats inside of them.

Because African Greys may chew on toys a lot, make sure the toys are made of safe, non-toxic materials. Sisal, natural fibers, and wooden toys are excellent choices; however, stay away from toys with little pieces that may be ingested or materials that might provide a choking danger.

Gathering Necessary Materials

To take care of your African Grey Parrot, you must acquire all the materials and set up the cage and surroundings. Before taking your bird home, make sure you have the following essentials ready:

1. Food and Water Dishes: Because they are bacterially resistant, long-lasting, and simple to clean, stainless steel bowls are the finest choice for food and water. Ensure that water, dry food, and fresh food are all served in different plates.

2. Diet and Nutrition: African Greys need a balanced diet that includes high-quality pellets, fresh fruits, vegetables, and sometimes seeds or nuts. Since pellets are a great source of vitamins and minerals, they should constitute the bulk of your bird's diet. To provide diversity and extra nutrients, fresh fruits and vegetables such as bell peppers, apples, carrots, and leafy greens should be served every day. It's critical to stay away from items like avocado, chocolate, caffeine, and alcohol that are poisonous to birds.

3. Cleaning Supplies: The health of your bird depends on the cleanliness of their cage. Stock up on paper or other absorbent materials to line the cage tray and cleaning supplies that are safe for birds. To clean the cage bars, perches, and toys, you'll also need a strong scrub brush and a spray bottle.

4. First-Aid Kit: It's a good idea to have a basic first-aid kit for birds on available in case of accidents. This should include supplies like bandages, tweezers, antiseptic solution, and styptic powder (to halt bleeding from small injuries). Learn the fundamentals of first aid for birds, and have the number of an avian veterinarian on hand for any unexpected situations.

Modifying Your Way of Life to Fit an African Grey

Adapting an African Grey Parrot into your household will probably include changing your daily schedule. Due to their strong social nature, African Greys need constant human connection in order to maintain their happiness and well-being. This entails setting out time every day for conversing, engaging in play, and teaching your bird. African Greys who don't get enough care may exhibit aggressive, shouting, or feather plucking behaviors.

You should create a daily schedule for your bird's feeding, cleaning, and sleeping arrangements in addition to spending quality time with it. Because they are creatures of habit, African Greys do best in environments with regular routines.

To guarantee the safety of your African Grey while they are not in their cage, it is imperative that you bird-proof your house. African Greys like exploring, but if left alone, they may get into trouble. When your bird is not in its cage, ensure sure all windows and doors are shut tightly, remove any poisonous plants, and cover electrical connections.

Final Thoughts

Although caring for an African Grey Parrot is a lot of work, your efforts will be rewarded with a happy and healthy bird. Your home should be safe, stimulating, and pleasant. You may create the conditions for a long and fulfilling connection with your African Grey by carefully choosing the ideal cage, offering plenty of stimulation, and modifying your lifestyle to suit the bird's social and emotional requirements. To make sure that you and your bird have a great experience right from the start, planning is essential. One of the most special and rewarding elements of owning a pet will be the friendship you'll have with your African Grey, but it all begins with preparing your house to accept your new family member.

CHAPTER 4:

COMPREHENDING AFRICAN GREY PARROT BEHAVIOR

African Grey Parrots are intriguing companions because of their complicated personalities and well-known intellect. But this intelligence also comes with a broad variety of behaviors, some of which might be difficult for owners to comprehend. This chapter will explore the normal characteristics of African Greys, including body language, communication patterns, and common behavioral issues and solutions. To ensure your parrot's general wellbeing and to establish a solid, good bond with them, it's important to comprehend these actions.

Social Connectivity and Nature

The very sociable component of African Grey behavior is one of its most significant features. These parrots live in big groups in the wild and are often interacting with one another. African Greys provide their human friends the same desire for socializing as they have as pets. They develop close relationships with their owners and often get quite devoted to one or two family members.

Owning an African Grey involves a wonderful bonding process, but it also implies that these birds are very sensitive to emotions. For mental stimulation and emotional stability, they depend on their social networks. Due to the fact that African Greys need constant attention, contact, and communication, owners must dedicate time to these activities on a regular basis. When these social demands are ignored, emotional pain may result, and unpleasant actions are often the result.

Interaction and Voiceovers

The remarkable ability of African Grey Parrots to imitate human speech and other noises is one of their most well-known characteristics. These parrots have the ability to amass a vocabulary of hundreds of words, making them among of the finest talkers among birds. Even more impressively, African Greys are renowned for utilizing words and phrases appropriately. For example, they may say "hello" to their owner or "come here" to get their attention.

Although many owners find great pleasure in their ability to imitate, it's crucial to realize that vocalization is an inherent aspect of their communication. African Greys utilize vocalizations to express themselves and convey their requirements, in addition to mimicking. They utilize sounds in the wild to communicate with other members of their flock, warn of danger, or convey their feelings. In their role as pets, they will similarly use a variety of noises to interact with their human "flock."

Typical vocalizations consist of:

- *Soft Talking and Chattering:* These are usually indicators of a contented and at ease bird. When your African Grey feels secure and at ease, you could hear it practice words and noises.

Auditory Calls or Screams: This is often an indication that your bird is nervous or is trying to get attention. If someone uses screaming as a method to grab your attention, it may become problematic. By responding to shouts, owners must refrain from encouraging this behavior. Rather than ignoring it, attempt to identify the root reason, whether it be stress, loneliness, or boredom.

- *Mimicking noises:* Due to their natural curiosity, African Greys will imitate noises from their surroundings, including phones, doorbells, and appliances in the home. Even while this might be amusing, it's crucial to provide them enough stimulus to keep them from becoming disengaged from imitation alone.

Body Language

African Greys express their emotions and intents via body language in addition to vocalizations. Understanding your parrot's mood and reacting accordingly requires that you learn to read their body language. The following are important body language clues to be aware of:

- *Fluffed Feathers:* There are a few different meanings associated with an African Grey's fluffed feathers. Your bird is probably happy and at ease if it fluffs its feathers before going to sleep or when it is calm. On the other hand, prolonged puffiness in the bird—especially if it is accompanied by lethargy—may indicate a medical condition.

- *Wings Spreading or Drooping:* A bird that seems to be expanding its wings and spreads them out is probably simply unwinding or cooling down. On the other hand, prolonged drooping or holding of the wings might be a sign of exhaustion or disease.

- *Tail Fanning:* When an African Grey spreads its tail feathers widely, it might be indicating excitement or aggression. Other indicators of excitement, such as dilated pupils and vocalizations, often accompany this activity.

- *Pupil Dilation (Eye Pinning):* The rapid contraction and dilation of an African Grey's pupil is referred to as "eye pinning." Usually, this happens when the bird is aroused, stimulated, or excited. It is crucial to pay attention to the environment in which this occurs. A bird may be preparing to bite if it is accompanied by hostile postures like lunging or flicking its tail.

- **Beak Grinding:** An African Grey's tendency to grind its beak indicates happiness and calm. Before going to bed, a lot of birds grind their beaks.

- **Head Bobbing or Bowing:** Head bobbing might be seen as a request for attention or as enthusiasm. A few birds even bowed their heads to be rubbed or touched.

Regrettably, Feather Plucking: Stress, boredom, or a lack of social engagement are often the causes of this widespread behavioral problem in African Greys. In order to determine any stresses, it's critical to assess your bird's habit and surroundings if you see it plucking feathers.

Behavioral Difficulties and Their Remedies

African Grey Parrots are gregarious and intelligent birds, but they may exhibit a variety of behavioral issues, especially when their emotional and environmental requirements aren't addressed. Feather plucking, aggressiveness, and excessive vocalizations are the most prevalent problems. You may address these habits before they worsen by being aware of their underlying causes.

Picking Feathers

Pulling off feathers is an unpleasant practice known as feather plucking, which often results in bald patches and even self-harm. Numerous things, such as stress, worry, boredom, dietary inadequacies, or disease, might contribute to it.

It's important to make sure your African Grey is receiving enough mental stimulation and social engagement in order to avoid or treat feather plucking. Give them plenty of toys, opportunity to forage, and daily one-on-one time. To rule out any health concerns, make sure the bird's food is well-balanced and speak with an avian veterinarian.

Try to find any environmental changes that could be stressing the bird out if feather plucking continues. This can include a new pet, home modifications, or even insufficient sleep.

Biting and Aggression

Another frequent problem with African Greys is aggression, which includes biting, particularly during hormonal times. Birds may bite as a result of territorial behavior, fear, or irritation. Building a trustworthy bond with your bird early on is essential to preventing biting. Respect your bird's limits at all times and refrain from pressuring encounters.

Training based on positive reinforcement has the potential to be very successful in deterring aggressive behavior. Reward your African Grey when they behave calmly and well; scolding them may exacerbate trust difficulties and create fear.

Overly Loud Voices

While little vocalization on the part of African Greys is acceptable and even preferred, excessive yelling might cause issues. Birds may scream in response to stress, boredom, or attention. The secret to dealing with excessive vocalizations is to avoid encouraging the behavior and instead provide plenty of enrichment. Don't react right away if your bird cries for attention, for instance, since this will teach them that shouting is a useful tactic for getting what they want. As an alternative, wait to react until the bird is quiet and peaceful to reinforce the concept that good deeds attract attention.

Final Thoughts

It's essential to comprehend your African Grey Parrot's behavior in order to provide them the finest care and maintain a positive, happy connection. Because they are very clever birds, owners must learn to read their signals because they communicate with them via vocalizations, body language, and gestures. Even though African Greys may have behavioral problems including feather plucking, aggressiveness, and excessive vocalization, these problems are often avoidable with the right upkeep, attention, and stimulation.

With an awareness of African Greys' social nature, an awareness of their communication styles, and early intervention for behavioral problems, you may help your parrot and you develop a solid, happy relationship. In exchange, your African Grey will bring you with friendship, amusement, and devotion for many years to come.

CHAPTER 5:

FURNISHING YOUR AFRICAN GREY PARROT WITH THE PERFECT ENVIRONMENT

One of the most crucial things in guaranteeing the health and happiness of your African Grey Parrot is to provide a well-organized and exciting environment. These birds are sociable and extremely clever animals that do best in rich surroundings that try to mimic the circumstances they would find in the wild. This chapter will go over the essential components of setting up the perfect house for your African Grey Parrot, such as selecting the appropriate cage, being aware of how much room they need, providing mental and physical stimulation, keeping things clean, and making their home a fun and safe place.

Selecting the Appropriate Cage

The African Grey Parrot's cage is the main component of its environment, thus choosing the proper one is essential to the health of your pet. African Greys are medium-to-large birds that need plenty of room to walk about, spread their wings, and exercise. As a result, one of the first things to think about should be the cage size.

- *Size:* Generally speaking, larger cages are preferable. A minimum cage size for an African Grey should be around 36 inches in length, 24 inches in width, and 48 inches in height. As a result, the bird may freely flap its wings without running afoul of the cage's sides. Additionally, the bars should be spaced no wider than ¾ to 1 inch apart to prevent your parrot from becoming caught or escaping.

- **Shape and Design:** It's critical to choose a cage that is both roomy and attractive. An excessively tall cage that is too small prevents the bird from having adequate horizontal room to roam about. African Greys love to climb, investigate, and engage with their surroundings, so having space in both the horizontal and vertical directions in their cage is perfect. Furthermore, the cage has to have strong locks since African Greys have a history of finding out how to open even the simplest latches.

- **Material:** Because African Grey Parrots are voracious chewers, the cage's material has to be robust. The best cages are made of stainless steel since it is not only durable but also rust-proof and clean-able. Steer clear of cages constructed of hazardous materials like lead or zinc, since they may cause injury to your parrot if consumed.

Configuring the Cage

Setting up your African Grey's cage to give comfort, stimulation, and safety comes next once you've chosen the ideal cage. Care should be used while designing the cage's interior to encourage both physical and mental health.

- *Perches:* Because they provide your parrot a place to rest and exercise their feet, perches are vital to their physical well-being. To replicate the branches they would utilize in the environment, use perches made of natural wood with different sizes. This variation keeps their feet healthy and protects against problems like arthritis and foot blisters. To keep your African Grey's cage hygienic, make sure the perches are positioned at various heights so that it may climb and explore, but don't put them directly over food or water bowls.

- *Food and Water Bowls:* Located in conveniently accessible sections of the cage are food and water bowls. The greatest choice are bowls made of stainless steel since they are robust and simple to maintain. To stop germs from growing and contamination, wash these dishes every day. In order to keep the water pure and free of food particles or waste, many parrot owners also utilize water bottles made specifically for parrots.

- *Toys and Enrichment:* Due to their intelligence, African Greys need mental stimulation to keep from becoming bored. A bored parrot is more prone to start acting out by yelling or pulling feathers. Offer a range of playthings, such as mirrors (under supervision), chewable toys, puzzle toys, and foraging toys. To make the space new and engaging, rotate the toys on a regular basis. Ladders and hanging swings may also inspire your bird to be active and give it a feeling of adventure.

- *Cage Location:* The location of your African Grey's cage in your house is just as crucial as the contents of the cage. Because birds like socializing, choose a spot where they can participate in everyday activities. But stay away from putting the cage in bright sunlight, drafts, or next to the kitchen where nonstick cookware odors might be dangerous. For these delicate birds, it is crucial to avoid unneeded stress by providing a calm, steady environment.

Ensuring Excitation of the Mind and Body

Known for their intellect, African Grey Parrots need mental stimulation every day to maintain their happiness and well-being. It's crucial to provide your parrot mentally and physically demanding activities in addition to toys and cage enrichment.

Out-of-Cage Time: In order to explore and engage with their surroundings, African Greys need time spent outside of their cage. Aim for two to three hours per day of supervised time spent outside of the cage. During this period, your parrot may play with toys or other family members, exercise, and extend its wings. During this time, you may also train your bird by giving them new orders, tricks, or phrases to increase their cognitive function.

- *Foraging:* It's critical to mimic African Greys' natural habit of foraging in captivity. Give your bird foraging devices that conceal food or treats so they will have to work for their meal. This helps avoid boredom-related behaviors like feather plucking and excessive vocalization in addition to keeping them intellectually occupied.

- *connection and Socialization:* African Greys are gregarious birds that crave for human connection. Spend time with your bird, talk to it often, and provide it socializing chances. When their owners are not there, some parrots like to watch television or listen to music. However, it's crucial to make sure they have enough one-on-one time with you so they may feel emotionally satisfied.

Preserving Hygiene and Tidiness

Maintaining a clean environment is critical to the health of your African Grey. Respiratory problems, bacterial or fungal infections, and general health problems might result from dirty cages. Here are some pointers for keeping your bird's environment hygienic and thriving:

- ***Daily Cleaning:*** Empty the food and water bowls, replenish the water, and remove any leftover food. To stop germs from growing, remove any waste or dirty bedding from the bottom of the cage.

- *Weekly Cleaning:* Wipe down the cage's bars with a combination of water and white vinegar or a bird-safe cleaner once a week for a more thorough cleaning. To eliminate dirt and debris, wash the toys, perches, and any other cage accessories. To maintain a lively and new atmosphere, turn over the toys and perches.

- *Deep Cleaning:* Disassemble the cage and give it a thorough cleaning every several months. After removing every accessory, thoroughly clean the cage and use a disinfectant that is suitable for birds. Before putting the cage back together, let everything dry thoroughly.

Establishing a Secure and Cozy Environment

Ensuring your African Grey's habitat is secure and pleasant is just as important as giving them mental stimulation and keeping it clean.

- **Temperature and Humidity:** Because African Grey Parrots are native to tropical locations, warm, somewhat humid weather is preferred by them. Maintain an indoor temperature of 65° to 80°F and stay away from drafts and abrupt temperature swings. In arid areas, you may also use a humidifier to keep the humidity at 50–60%, which is good for the skin and respiratory system of your parrot.

- **Sleep Environment:** African Greys need 10 to 12 hours of sleep per night, just like any other parrot. Put the cage in a room that stays dark at night or cover it to create a peaceful, dark sleeping space. Making sure your parrot gets adequate sleep can help shield it from behavioral problems and stress.

- *Safety Considerations:* Because they are inquisitive creatures, African Greys will investigate both the inside and outside of their cage. It's critical to parrot-proof your house by getting rid of any possible threats, such tiny, ingestible items, electrical wires, and poisonous plants. When your bird is outside of its cage, always keep an eye on it to avoid mishaps or injury.

Final Thoughts

It takes more than just a cage to provide your African Grey Parrot with the perfect home. It involves establishing an atmosphere that promotes their mental, emotional, and physical well. You can guarantee that your African Grey flourishes in captivity by selecting the ideal cage, providing enough stimulation, keeping your house tidy, and making sure your pet feels secure and at ease. In addition to keeping your parrot healthy and happy, a well-designed environment can help you and your bird develop a strong, enduring relationship.

CHAPTER 6:

RECOGNIZING AND FULFILLING THE NUTRITIONAL REQUIREMENTS OF YOUR AFRICAN GREY

One of the most crucial parts of taking care of your African Grey Parrot is feeding them a healthy diet. Similar to us, African Greys need a balanced diet to be as healthy, active, and long as possible. A diet deficient in vital nutrients may cause a number of health issues, including as obesity, feather plucking, malnutrition, and even potentially fatal diseases like vitamin deficiencies or fatty liver disease. This chapter will discuss the unique dietary requirements of African Grey Parrots, such as what kinds of foods they should consume, how important diversity is, and how to control their diet for long-term well-being.

A Balanced Diet's Significance

The African Grey Parrot is a highly clever bird with complex nutritional requirements. They may find a vast range of food items in the environment, including as seeds, nuts, fruits, vegetables, and even tiny insects. To keep them healthy in captivity, it is essential to replicate this variation. Your parrot will obtain the proper quantities of vitamins, minerals, proteins, fats, and carbs from a balanced meal, supporting both their physical and mental health.

- Variety is Key: Offering a diverse meal to your African Grey is one of the most crucial feeding guidelines. An over reliance on a single food item, like seeds, in a diet may result in nutritional imbalances. To suit their dietary demands, African Greys need a variety of fresh fruits and vegetables along with grains, seeds, nuts, and premium pellets. Providing diversity at mealtimes keeps your parrot interested and stimulated while also ensuring that your bird receives all the nutrition it needs.

Structures as the Basis: Your African Grey's food should be based mostly on well prepared pellets. These pellets are a great method to make sure your parrot receives the vitamins and minerals it needs since they are made particularly to provide a balanced blend of nutrients. Your parrot's food should consist of 60–70% pellets. However, because artificial colors, tastes, and preservatives might eventually hurt your bird, it's crucial to choose pellets devoid of these ingredients.

Fresh Vegetables and Fruits

Fresh fruits and vegetables are a vital part of an African Grey's diet in addition to pellets. They provide essential vitamins, minerals, and antioxidants that boost the health of the feathers, the immune system, and general wellbeing.

- *Vegetables:* Due to their propensity for calcium deficiency, African Greys, in particular, benefit greatly from eating dark, leafy greens like kale, spinach, and collard greens. Carrots, bell peppers, broccoli, and squash are some other nutrient-dense veggies. They provide a variety of vitamins, including vitamin A, which is essential for healthy eyes and a strong immune system.

- *Fruits:* Natural sugars and vitamins may be found in fruits including berries, bananas, apples, and papayas. Fruits should, however, be consumed in moderation because of their high sugar content. Your African Grey's diet should consist of 20–25% veggies and 10–15% fruits. Before giving any fruits or veggies to your parrot, always make sure they have been completely cleaned to get rid of any chemicals or pesticides.

- *Safe and Innocent Foods:* Although a lot of fruits and vegetables are good for African Greys, some should be avoided as they might be poisonous to them. Persin, for instance, is found in avocados and may be fatal to parrots. Garlic, onions, and rhubarb are also toxic. Fruit pits and seeds (from peaches, cherries, and apples, for example) should always be removed before feeding since they contain poisonous chemicals called cyanogenic compounds.

Nuts, Grains, and Seeds

Although nuts and seeds are often included in parrot meals, their high fat content should only be tolerated in small amounts. Although these meals are enjoyed by African Greys, eating too much of them may result in obesity, fatty liver disease, and other health issues. But when consumed in moderation, they provide vital proteins and lipids.

- *Seeds:* Although they shouldn't comprise a large portion of your African Grey's diet, you may sometimes give them treats or include seeds into their meal. A diet limited to seeds is very unbalanced and may cause malnourishment. For example, sunflower seeds are heavy in fat and should be given in moderation.

- *Nuts:* Nuts are heavy in fat yet rich in nutrients, much like seeds. Pistachios, walnuts, and almonds may be given as prizes or occasional snacks throughout training. Nuts are an excellent source of proteins and healthy fats as well, but moderation is crucial since overfeeding them may cause weight problems.

Grains and Legumes: You may feed your African Grey a diet rich in carbohydrates by using grains like quinoa, brown rice, and oats. Cooked legumes, such as beans, lentils, and chickpeas, are also advantageous because they include important fiber and proteins. Before giving these grains and legumes to your parrot, always make sure they are well cooked and devoid of any additional salts, oils, or seasonings.

Vitamin and Calcium Supplements

Given their propensity for calcium deficiency, African Grey Parrots need a lot of calcium in their diet. Low calcium levels may cause problems including weak bones, female egg binding, and even convulsions. Give your parrot meals high in calcium, such as leafy greens, and calcium supplements if needed to make sure it receives enough of the mineral.

- **_Minestral Blocks and Cuttlebones:_** These are great places to get calcium and other minerals. Additionally, they help your parrot maintain the health of its beak. Give your parrot access to a mineral block or cuttlebone in its cage, and change it out as required.

- **_Vitamin D:_** When exposed to sunshine, African Greys may naturally synthesize vitamin D, which is important for the absorption of calcium. That being said, your parrot could not be receiving enough sunshine if it spends the majority of its time inside. You may give your bird vitamin D pills, make sure it receives some sunshine, or use UV lights specifically made for birds.

Water Quality and Hydration

A healthy diet is crucial, but so is maintaining enough hydrated. Give your African Grey access to clean, fresh water at all times. Since parrots often immerse their food in their water, which might promote bacterial development, it is important to change the water every day to avoid contamination. Water bottles made specifically for parrots are preferred by some parrot owners since they may prolong the life of the water's cleanliness.

- *Avoid Sugary or Caffeinated Beverages:* Although it might be tempting to give your parrot drinks like soda or juice, it's best to refrain from doing so. These may be detrimental to the health of your bird and may also be a factor in obesity and other health problems.

Controlling Food Consumption to Prevent Overfeeding

African Greys may exhibit selective feeding, which is the tendency to pick out their preferred meals and disregard the others, or overeating. It's critical to keep an eye on their food consumption and make sure they're eating a balanced diet to avoid this. Food should not be left in the cage all day as this might encourage overindulgence and obesity. Rather, serve meals on a regular basis and take out any food that isn't consumed within a few hours.

- *Portion Control:* Because your African Grey's nutritional demands vary according on their age, activity level, and general health, it may be difficult to determine how much food they should be consuming. Offering ¼ to ½ cup of pellets every day, augmented with fresh fruits and vegetables and sometimes seeds or nuts, is a good general guideline.

Rewarding Training and Treats

In addition to being a wonderful method to strengthen your relationship, treats may also be helpful during training. Still, their share of your parrot's food shouldn't exceed 5%. Small bits of fruit, unsalted almonds, or specially prepared parrot snacks are examples of healthy reward alternatives. Treating your parrot with high-sugar or high-fat human meals might be detrimental to their health.

Final Thoughts

For your African Grey Parrot to have a long, healthy, and happy life, you must provide for its dietary requirements. You can provide your parrot the nutrition it needs to flourish by providing a diverse, balanced diet that includes premium pellets, fresh fruits and vegetables, and sometimes seeds and nuts. Always keep in mind that diversity and moderation are the keys to avoiding nutritional imbalances, and keep an eye on your bird's food to make sure it's keeping them in good overall health and weight. An African Grey will live a long and healthy life if it is fed well and receives frequent veterinarian care.

CHAPTER 7:

GIVING YOUR AFRICAN GREY EXERCISE, PLAY, AND ENRICHMENT

An essential part of taking care of your African Grey Parrot is providing mental and physical stimulation. For these bright, energetic birds to flourish in captivity, they need mental and physical stimulation. African Greys are prone to behavioral problems including boredom, feather plucking, and even depression if they don't have enough stimulus. The present chapter focuses on the significance of offering chances for physical activity, play, and cerebral stimulation to your bird, since these activities are vital for preserving its general welfare.

The Significance of Exercise

African Grey Parrots are inherently energetic birds that mostly engage in flying, climbing, and foraging throughout their time in the wild. Regular exercise is crucial since they have less opportunity to participate in these natural activities when they are in captivity. Exercise supports the growth of muscles, aids in maintaining a healthy weight, and improves cardiovascular health in general.

- *Flight Time:* Flying is one of the best ways for an African Grey to exercise. It is quite advantageous to let your parrot fly in a secure, supervised area if you have decided to keep its wings unclipped. Within your house, set aside a space for your bird to fly short distances and spread its wings. Make sure there are no risks in the area, such as ceiling fans, open windows, or other hazards.

- ***Climbing and Perching:*** You may promote exercise in your parrot even if its wings are clipped by giving it chances to climb and perch. African Greys get strength in their legs and beaks while climbing on trees, ladders, and ropes. To promote mobility and foot activity, provide a range of perches in their cage, each with a varied height and texture. Because natural hardwood perches have a more diverse feel than slick plastic ones, they are especially beneficial for preserving the health of your feet.

- ***Toys for Physical Activity:*** Another great technique to encourage fitness is using toys that stimulate movement. Ladders, ropes, and swings are all excellent ways to encourage your parrot to explore its surroundings. Additionally, you may add foraging toys, which mix cerebral and physical engagement by requiring your bird to climb or move in order to get goodies.

Enhancing Cognitive Function and Mental Stimulation

For African Greys, mental stimulation is just as crucial as physical training. These very clever parrots may become dissatisfied or bored if they don't get adequate mental challenges. They spend a lot of time in the wild interacting with their surroundings and searching for food, so emulating similar behaviors in captivity keeps them occupied.

- Foraging Toys: Using foraging toys is one of the finest methods to provide your African Grey mental stimulation. These toys encourage your bird to forage for food, mimicking the natural habits of foraging. Your parrot will have to figure out how to get to the reward if you conceal tiny treats or food particles within the toy. There are many different kinds of foraging toys, ranging from simple puzzles to intricate devices that need critical thinking.

- Interactive Toys: Puzzle toys and other toys that need interaction from your African Grey are excellent sources of cerebral stimulation. These toys often require the user to spin wheels, pull levers, or push buttons in order to obtain a

reward. These kinds of toys may keep African Greys entertained for hours on end and help them avoid boredom, as they are recognized for their ability to solve problems.

Training Sessions: Another great method to stimulate your African Grey's thinking is to have regular training sessions. In addition to improving the relationship between you and your parrot, teaching it new skills or orders gives it important mental stimulation. Training using rewards or praise when your bird exhibits a desired behavior is known as positive reinforcement, and it works especially well. Your parrot may be trained to utter words or phrases, wave, and even retrieve stuff.

Social Engagement and Cultivation

The relationship between African Greys and their human partners is immensely beneficial to them as social birds. They belong to big groups in the wild and spend a lot of time chatting and associating with other birds. They need frequent social connection to feel safe and comfortable in a home setting.

- *Daily Engagement:* Engage in conversation with your African Grey each day. This might include conversing with your bird, providing toys for it, or doing training sessions. African Greys are noted for their capacity to imitate human speech, and consistent conversation with your bird can help it grow into a more talkative bird. Furthermore, spending time with your parrot strengthens your relationship with it and lowers the risk of behavioral problems like aggressiveness or anxiety.

- ***Rotating Toys and Activities:*** It's critical to routinely rotate your African Grey's toys and activities to keep it entertained. If birds are kept in their cages for extended periods of time, they may become bored with the same toys. You can maintain an interesting and engaging environment for your parrot by switching out the toys in its cage every few weeks or by adding new ones. To create fresh challenges, you may even rearrange the toys or perches inside the cage.

Avoiding Behavioral Problems and Boredom

One of the most frequent reasons African Greys have behavioral issues is boredom. Your bird may turn to unpleasant habits like feather plucking, excessive screaming, or destructive chewing if it doesn't get enough mental and physical activity. You can aid in preventing these problems and maintaining your parrot's mental and physical well-being by giving it a wide range of toys, activities, and social contact.

- *Feather Plucking:* A typical behavioral problem in African Greys, feather plucking is often an indication of boredom, stress, or dissatisfaction. Enough toys and social engagement to stimulate the mind enough may help stop this habit. In the event that your parrot starts plucking feathers, assess its surroundings to make sure it receives enough exercise, mental stimulation, and socialization.

Chewing: African Greys have a natural drive to chew; giving them items that they may safely gnaw on can help satiate this urge. To encourage healthy chewing activity, wooden toys, branches appropriate for birds, and foraging toys are all excellent choices. Don't give your parrot poisonous or plastic objects to chew on since they might be dangerous if consumed.

CHAPTER 8:

GETTING TO KNOW YOUR AFRICAN GREY AND FORMING BONDS

The secret to your African Grey Parrot's pleasure and general wellbeing is to develop a close relationship with it. These birds are very gregarious and develop close emotional bonds with the people who look after them. But developing a relationship with an African Grey takes persistence, patience, and time. This chapter will cover bonding strategies, the value of socializing, and building trust with your bird.

Socialization's Significance

In the wild, African Grey Parrots flourish in flocks due to their innate gregarious nature. Since you become their flock while they are in captivity, socializing is essential to their mental and emotional well. African Greys are susceptible to behavioral problems including aggressiveness, fearfulness, and excessive screaming if they are not socialized properly. Socialization strengthens the link between you and your parrot while assisting your bird in feeling safe and at ease in its surroundings.

- ***Early socializing:*** It's crucial to start early socializing with your young African Grey. Positively and carefully introduce your bird to a range of people, places, and activities. This promotes socialization and reduces the likelihood of fear-based behavior in your parrot. It's crucial to go cautiously and avoid giving your bird too much at once. Your parrot will develop confidence if they are gradually introduced to new experiences.

- **Building Trust:** A solid relationship with your African Grey starts with building trust. Positive encounters that are consistent help to build trust. Spend some time chatting to your bird in a soothing, quiet voice while you're near its cage. When your parrot comes up to you or shows interest in engaging, give it some goodies and soft words of encouragement. Steer clear of abrupt movements and loud sounds as they may startle your bird and undermine the trust you have worked so hard to establish.

Creating a Bond with Routine

Establishing a solid relationship with your African Grey requires consistency. Since parrots like consistency, scheduling regular feedings, training sessions, and playtimes can make your bird feel safe and at ease. Establishing a consistent daily schedule not only improves the relationship with your bird but also lessens tension and worry.

Daily Interaction: Establish the daily routine of spending time with your African Grey. Your relationship with your bird may be strengthened just by spending time together, having conversations, or giving it a favorite toy. Formal training sessions are not necessarily necessary. Because African Greys are sociable creatures and are very clever, your relationship with your parrot will only become stronger the more time you spend with them.

- *Handling and Physical Contact:* Treating your African Grey with gentleness fosters trust and fortifies your relationship. To get your bird to approach you, start by giving it delicacies right out of your hand. You may start giving your parrot your hand to walk on after it feels at ease with you. Handle your bird with gentleness and respect at all times, since coercing physical contact may erode trust and breed fear or aggressiveness.

Establishing a Good Connection

Respect, trust, and understanding between you and your African Grey are the cornerstones of a healthy partnership. It's crucial to approach your relationships with your parrot with compassion and empathy since they turn to you for direction, care, and friendship.

- *Positive Reinforcement:* To promote desired actions, use positive reinforcement strategies. When your bird exhibits a desired action, such walking onto your palm or obeying a command, reward it with sweets, praise, or your undivided attention. Negative reinforcement and punishment should be avoided since they might weaken your relationship and encourage fear-based conduct.

- *Respecting Boundaries:* African Greys are individuals with unique personalities and interests, much like people. While some birds may prefer less physical contact, others may appreciate being handled regularly. Respecting your bird's limits and avoiding pressuring it to engage if it seems anxious or uncomfortable are key. Respecting your parrot's wants and preferences can help you develop a closer, more reliable bond.

bind.

Handling the Anxiety of Separation

Strong emotional ties between African Grey Parrots and their human caregivers are well recognized, and this may sometimes cause separation anxiety. Your parrot may exhibit nervous behaviors, including excessive shrieking, plucking of feathers, or destructive chewing, if it is left alone for extended periods of time.

- *Creating a Comfortable Environment:* Provide your African Grey with a stimulating and comfortable environment to help them cope with separation anxiety. Give your bird plenty of toys, perches, and food sources to keep them busy while you're gone. A low-volume radio or television may also offer background noise, which will make your parrot feel less lonely.

- *Gradual Separation Training:* You may help your African Grey get more used to being by yourself if it suffers from separation anxiety. Begin by spending brief amounts of time apart from your bird and progressively extend that time. To keep your parrot occupied while you are away, always make sure it has a plenty of mental and physical stimulation.

Final Thoughts

An important part of caring for African Grey Parrots is socialization and bonding. These very sensitive and clever birds need to feel safe in their connection with their human caregivers since they thrive on contact. A lifetime of strong and trusting attachment may be formed between you and your African Grey by giving consistent, pleasant experiences, honoring your bird's limits, and controlling separation anxiety.

CHAPTER 9:

AFRICAN GREY PARROT HEALTH AND COMMON ILLNESSES

Understanding and preserving an African Grey Parrot's health is an essential part of caring for them. These perceptive avians are renowned for their extended lifespans—they often survive in captivity for 40–60 years or beyond. It's essential to be knowledgeable about your parrot's health requirements, prevalent illnesses, and preventive care techniques in order to guarantee its long-term success. A thorough review of the health issues pertaining to African Grey Parrots is given in this chapter, which also addresses common illnesses, symptoms of sickness, diet, and routine veterinarian treatment.

Nutrition's Significance to Health

African Grey Parrot health is based on eating a balanced diet. These birds need a diversified diet that satisfies their nutritional requirements and boosts their immune system and general health. A healthy diet need to include:

1. Pellets: The mainstay of your African Grey's food should be well prepared pellets. The purpose of these pellets is to provide balanced amounts of vital vitamins, minerals, and other nutrients. Select pellets made especially for medium-to large-sized parrots or African Greys;

stay away from pellets with artificial tastes or colors.

2. *Fresh Fruits and Vegetables:* Additional vitamins and minerals may only be obtained from fresh food. Every day, provide a range of fruits and vegetables, including bell peppers, apples, bananas, carrots, and leafy greens. Make sure all fruits and veggies are well cleaned and sliced into little pieces. Steer clear of harmful foods like chocolate, avocado, and coffee.

3. *Seeds and Nuts:* Because of their high fat content, seeds and nuts should not comprise more than 10% to 15% of your parrot's diet, even if they may be given as rewards. Select unseasoned and unsalted choices, and think about distributing nuts such as walnuts, sunflower seeds, and almonds sparingly.

4. Water: Always have access to fresh, clean water. To make sure the water doesn't become contaminated, change it every day.

5. Supplements: Dietary supplements could be required in certain circumstances, particularly if your parrot isn't eating a balanced diet. To find out whether your African Grey needs supplements like calcium, vitamin D3, or omega-3 fatty acids, speak with your veterinarian.

Ongoing Veterinary Treatment

Veterinary examinations on a regular basis are essential to keeping your African Grey healthy. Form a connection with an avian veterinarian who specializes in the treatment of birds. Annual physical examinations must to comprise:

- ***Physical Examinations:*** A comprehensive check-up to determine the weight, general look, and feather condition of your parrot.

- ***Fecal Tests:*** A fecal examination for bacterial illnesses and parasites.

- ***Blood Tests:*** Blood tests to track possible health problems, nutritional status, and organ function.

- ***Wing and Beak Care:*** Consistently check to make sure the beak is healthy and the wings are trimmed properly.

Effective treatment of health disorders requires early identification. See a veterinarian right once if you see any changes in your parrot's appearance, behavior, or hunger.

Common ailments that affect African Grey Parrots

Many of the ailments that African Grey Parrots are prone to may be avoided or controlled with the right treatment. The following are some typical health concerns to be aware of:

1. Parrot fever, or pustacosis: Both people and birds may get psittacosis, which is brought on by the bacteria Chlamydia psittaci. Lethargy, diarrhea, and respiratory discomfort are among the symptoms. Contact with respiratory secretions or contaminated droppings may spread this illness. Antibiotics are usually used as a form of treatment, and sick birds should be kept in isolation to stop the illness from spreading.

2. Atherosclerosis: A high-fat diet is often linked to the accumulation of plaque in the arteries that causes this cardiovascular disease. Suggested symptoms might include fatigue, dyspnea, and unexpected death. Prevention requires a heart-healthy diet, consistent exercise, and weight control.

3. weight: Heart disease and arthritis are among the health problems that African Grey Parrots are susceptible to because to their weight. Obesity may be caused by an excessively fat diet, inactivity, and overfeeding. Keep an eye on your bird's weight and modify its food and exercise schedule appropriately.

4. *Feather-Plucking:* Health issues, boredom, or stress may all contribute to this activity. Affected birds may pluck their feathers, which may result in skin infections and bald patches. In order to address underlying health concerns, treatment frequently consists of veterinarian care, environmental enrichment, and behavioral modification.

5. *Respiratory Infections:* Smoke, drafts, and poor air quality are some of the environmental variables that may cause respiratory infections in African Grey Parrots. Breathing difficulties, nasal discharge, and wheezing are among the symptoms. Treatment requires immediate veterinarian attention.

6. *Egg-Binding:* An egg that becomes stuck in the reproductive canal is a problem that may happen to female African Grey Parrots. Lethargy, straining, and swollen abdomen are symptoms. Veterinarian assistance is required immediately since this illness has the potential to be fatal.

7. *Gastrointestinal Disorders:* African Greys are susceptible to a number of gastrointestinal disorders, including as bacterial or fungal infections, crop infections, and dietary-related concerns. Changes in appetite, vomiting, and diarrhea are possible symptoms. Timely veterinarian treatment and routine monitoring are essential.

Indices of Disease

It's essential to identify sickness symptoms in your African Grey in order to take prompt action. Typical indicators to look out for include:

- *Changes in Appetite:* Sudden changes in appetite, either more or less, may be a sign of medical problems. Keep a tight eye on your parrot's food schedule.

- *Changes in Behavior:* Aggression, lethargy, or social disengagement may be signs of disease or stress.

Changes in Vocalization: A shift in the vocalization's frequency or character might be a sign of unease or anxiety.

Physical Changes: Keep an eye out for symptoms like feather loss, altered droppings, puffiness, or strange movements.

For a comprehensive assessment and suitable care, get advice from a veterinarian if you see any of these symptoms.

Preventive Care Interventions

Maintaining the health of your African Grey Parrot requires preventative care. The following actions may be taken to guarantee the continued health of your bird:

Maintain Cleanliness: To avoid the growth of germs and parasites, clean your parrot's cage, toys, and food bowls on a regular basis.

Maintaining a clean atmosphere is essential to preventing sickness.

- Create a Stimulating Environment: To keep your African Grey from being bored or stressed, make sure it has plenty of enrichment activities. A bird that receives enough stimulation is less likely to have behavioral difficulties or health concerns linked to stress.

Weight and Health: Weigh your parrot on a regular basis and keep an eye on its general well-being. Maintaining a record of your bird's weight, food, and behavior can enable you to spot any changes that could point to a medical problem.

- *Educate Yourself:* Keep up to date on health concerns pertaining to African Greys and recommended methods of treatment. Gaining knowledge may help you keep your parrot happy and healthy.

Final Thoughts

Your African Grey Parrot's well-being and enjoyment of life are greatly dependent on its health. You can contribute to the longevity and well-being of your feathery companion by giving them a balanced food, making sure they get routine veterinarian treatment, and being informed about common illnesses and symptoms. Prevention is the key, and you can create an environment that supports your African Grey's health and happiness by being proactive.

CHAPTER 10:

AFRICAN GREY PARROT TRAINING

The rewarding experience of training an African Grey Parrot not only improves the relationship between you and your pet but also stimulates your mind. African Greys are renowned for their intelligence and capacity to pick up a wide range of skills and habits. The fundamentals of training African Grey Parrots, practical methods, and the advantages of training for you and your parrot are all covered in this chapter.

Recognizing the Intelligence of the African Grey

Among the smartest bird species are said to be African Grey Parrots. Their mental capacities are on par with those of some primates. They are quite trainable due to their intellect, but in order to keep their minds active and challenged, they need regular mental stimulation. It's important to understand your African Grey's learning style, motives, and natural habits in order to educate it properly.

Positive Reinforcement's Significance

A key component of training is positive reinforcement, which provides incentives for desired behavior. This approach improves the learning environment and deepens your relationship with your parrot. Key elements of training with positive reinforcement include the following:

- *Rewards:* Show love, praise, or goodies to encourage desired behavior. To keep your bird engaged, give it little, wholesome treats that are diverse in flavor. Fruit, vegetable, or specially prepared bird snacks are a few examples.

Timing: It's important to reinforce right away. As soon as your African Grey exhibits the required behavior, give them the incentive. This aids in the bird's association of the action with the gain.

- *Consistency:* Maintain a regular schedule for your workouts and awards. To reinforce learning, use the same signals and incentives for different actions.

- *Patience:* Every bird learns differently, so training takes time. Allow your African Grey to grow at a reasonable pace while exercising patience.

Fundamental Training Methods

The following methods should be included in your African Grey training regimen:

1. Clicker Training: Clicker training is a well-liked technique that marks the desired behavior with a little device that clicks. Click the gadget when your parrot does the behavior, and then give them a reward right away. Your bird will eventually learn to link the click sound with being rewarded.

2. *Target Training:* This method teaches your parrot to use its beak to contact an object, such your finger or a stick. To begin, place the target close to your bird's beak and give it a reward when it touches it. Increase the target cues' complexity and distance gradually.

3. *Shaping:* *Shaping entails dissecting an intricate behavior.*

Into more manageable stages. When your bird begins to approximate the necessary behavior, reward it. Gradually increase the specificity of the behaviors required before rewarding it. For instance, you may give your African Grey a treat for just approaching your hand rather of rewarding it for really stepping up onto it.

4. *Socialization* : Gradually expose your African Grey to new situations, people, and experiences. Positive socializing builds your bird's confidence and helps to lessen fear and anxiety. Reward your parrot for maintaining composure in novel circumstances.

Advanced Methods of Training

To keep your African Grey cognitively engaged, after they have learned basic instructions, you may introduce more complex training methods:

1. Tricks: Educating your parrot tricks is an enjoyable method to keep its mind occupied. Tricks like spinning, waving, and faking dead are common. When your parrot gains proficiency, progressively increase the difficulty of the tricks to help your bird learn new ones. Use positive reinforcement to help your bird learn new tricks.

2. *Vocalization:* The capacity to imitate words and sounds is a well-known trait of African Grey Parrots. Reward your bird for imitating you by rewarding it with repetitions of words and phrases to encourage vocalization. To keep the training interesting, use a range of noises and expressions.

3. *Obstacle Courses:* Using secure, bird-friendly materials, construct a basic obstacle course. Reward your African Grey after it completes each section to encourage it to continue through the course. Engaging in this pastime encourages both mental and physical activity.

4. Problem-Solving Activities: Give your parrot toys or puzzles that call for problem-solving abilities. These activities reduce boredom and possible behavioral problems by testing your bird's intellect and provide amusement.

Dealing with Behavioral Problems

Another useful method for treating typical behavioral problems in African Grey Parrots is training. The following are some tactics:

- ***Biting:*** You should take immediate action if your parrot starts biting. Recognize the causes of the biting and keep your bird out of circumstances that make it act out. Give it a toy to focus on instead, or give it praise for being quiet.

- *Screaming:* Some owners may find excessive vocalization to be alarming. Determine the source of the screaming, such as boredom, attention-seeking, or fear, to stop it. Use interactive play and enrichment activities to constructively channel your bird's energy.

- *Destructive Behavior:* When bored or nervous, African Greys may gnaw on or damage objects. Give your bird plenty of suitable toys and activities to keep them occupied. If your parrot starts acting destructively, reroute it to a toy that is acceptable for it and give it a treat for gnawing on the right things.

Strengthening the Link Through Training

Not only can you teach your African Grey orders and tricks, but training offers you the chance to forge a close relationship with your pet. The following advice can help you improve your connection while in training:

Interactive Sessions: Make sure that training sessions are interactive, brief, and interesting. To keep your parrot focused and enthusiastic, aim for ten to fifteen minute sessions a few times a day.

- *Respect Boundaries:* Be mindful of your bird's cues and body language. It's important to respect your African Grey's limits and give it a break if it exhibits indications of stress or apathy.

Appreciate Progress: Honor your parrot's accomplishments, no matter how little. Acknowledge and encourage your bird's progress to keep it learning.

Final Thoughts

Aside from improving your bond with your African Grey Parrot, training them is a fulfilling activity that encourages good behavior and cerebral stimulation. You may promote a happy and satisfying relationship with your bird by using positive reinforcement, figuring out your bird's preferred method of learning, and dealing with behavioral problems. A well-behaved African Grey may thrive in a caring home and is not only a delight to have, but it's also a healthier and happier bird. Both you and your feathery buddy will profit for the rest of your lives from the time and effort you put into their training.

CHAPTER 11:

AFRICAN GREY PARROT ENRICHMENT AND ACTIVITIES

African Grey Parrots are renowned for their extraordinary curiosity and intelligence. It is crucial to give children with an atmosphere that satisfies their mental, physical, and emotional requirements if you want to keep them happy and healthy. Activities and enrichment are essential to ensure African Greys have happy, fulfilled lives. This chapter explores the several ways you may improve the environment around your parrot, the value of stimulation, and the kinds of activities you can do to keep your bird occupied and happy.

Recognizing the Need for Improvement

African Grey Parrots in the wild spend their days searching for food, investigating their surroundings, and interacting with other birds. However, they often experience restrictions in captivity, which may cause stress, boredom, and behavioral issues. It is thus essential for their wellbeing to provide an atmosphere that is exciting and similar to their natural habitat. Engaging in physical, social, and cognitive activities are just a few ways that enrichment may manifest.

- ***Physical Enrichment:*** Offering chances for exercise and mobility is a kind of physical enrichment. In order to exercise and spread their wings, African Greys need room. Giving your bird a roomy cage filled with toys, climbing frames, and different perches will encourage it to go around and investigate.

- *Social Enrichment:* African Greys' mental health depends on their social connections. These birds love company, whether it comes from other birds or their human caretakers. Playing, chatting, and spending quality time with your parrot may improve your relationship and provide emotional support. Make sure your birds have enough opportunity to socialize with one another without being too dominant if you have more than one.

- *Cognitive Enrichment:* This kind of enrichment includes mental exercises for your parrot. African Greys are intellectual animals who take pleasure in challenges and problem-solving. Providing them with interactive games, puzzle toys, and foraging opportunities may help to keep their wits busy and sharp.

Classes of Activities for Enrichment

To encourage enrichment, you may add a variety of activities to your African Grey's daily schedule. Here are some concepts to think about:

1. Foraging Toys: Foraging is a natural habit for birds, and it may be quite helpful to provide toys that support this inclination. Seek for toys that let you conceal little quantities of food or goodies. By doing this, you may help your parrot become more like a wild forager by encouraging it to work for its food. You may also make your own foraging toys by wrapping or encasing goodies in cardboard boxes.

2. *Interactive Games:* Challenge your African Grey's intellect with interactive games. Multiple-step toys or toys that must be manipulated in order to get a reward may be very engaging. Toys that require the bird to access compartments, puzzle toys, and toys that dispense treats are a few common choices.

3. *Training Sessions:* Training is a great method to cognitively challenge your African Grey and reinforce good behavior. To teach your bird new orders or skills, use positive reinforcement methods like clicker training. Together with mental stimulation, training fortifies your relationship. You should keep your parrot's attention by keeping sessions brief and enjoyable.

4. *Toy Rotation:* If birds have access to the same toys for long stretches of time, they may become bored with them. To keep your African Grey's toys interesting and new, rotate them often. To keep the space engaging, occasionally introduce new toys and replace older ones.

5. *Sensory Stimulation:* A wide range of sensory stimuli are enjoyable to African Greys. Change the odors, sounds, and textures of their surroundings. You may give them noisy toys, crinkly paper for shredding, or real branches for perching. Verify that all items are non-toxic and safe.

6. outside Time: If it's practicable and safe, think about giving your African Grey some supervised outside time. Your bird's general health and temperament may be greatly enhanced by exposure to fresh air and natural sunshine. To make sure your parrot is safe while it's outside, use a bird leash or a sturdy aviary.

7. Social Interactions: As was previously indicated, African Greys need socializing. Plan frequent playtime for your bird to engage with you or other family members outside of the cage. Your parrot's social skills and emotional well-being may be improved by talking, singing, and engaging in games.

Value of Regular

Even though enrichment requires diversity, your African Grey may benefit from having a regular schedule. Because they are naturally predictable creatures, birds might feel more secure when their feeding, playing, and social schedules are well-established. Think about adding the following components to your daily routine:

- *Feeding plan :* Adhere to a regular feeding plan, providing clean water and new food at the same time every day. This schedule promotes good feeding habits and helps your bird anticipate meals.

Playtime: Designate certain periods of time for engagement and play. By doing this, you can make sure your parrot gets the care it needs and strengthen your relationship.

- **_Silent Time:_** Rest periods are just as important as active play. Give your African Grey some quiet time in its cage so it can unwind and recover without being bothered all the time.

Dealing with Behavioral Issues

African Grey Parrot behavioral problems include feather plucking, excessive screaming, and hostility might be caused by a lack of stimulation. Creating an atmosphere that is exciting might help lessen these issues. If you see your parrot acting out, check its surroundings for indications of dissatisfaction or boredom. These problems are often resolved by upping enrichment activities and making sure your bird has enough mental and physical activity.

Final Thoughts

An essential part of caring for African Grey Parrots is enrichment. It's possible to establish a happy and healthy atmosphere for them by recognizing their need for mental, physical, and social stimulation. You may raise a happy and well-adjusted companion by providing a range of enrichment activities, creating a schedule, and paying close attention to your bird's requirements. An African Grey parrot with a rich background is content and able to display its bright personality and intellect.

CHAPTER 12:

COMPREHENDING AFRICAN GREY COMMUNICATION AND BEHAVIOR

Forging a close relationship with your feathery friend requires an understanding of African Grey Parrot behavior and communication. These birds have high levels of social intelligence, and their actions often mirror their psychological and emotional states. You may better satisfy your parrot's requirements and create a pleasant connection by learning to read its body language, vocalizations, and social signs.

African Grey Parrots' Social Nature

Due to their innate social nature, African Grey Parrots exhibit behaviors that are greatly impacted by the social systems within which they live. These birds live in flocks in the wild, where they depend on one another for social interaction, safety, and friendship. They need to be socialized with their human caretakers in order to mimic this flock dynamic when maintained as pets.

- *Human Bonding:* African Greys are renowned for developing close relationships with their owners. Their mental health depends on this relationship. Play, training, and engagement with your parrot all contribute to the development of trust and strengthening of this relationship. Positive actions and vocalizations are more likely to be shown by an African Grey that is well-bonded.

- *Seeking Interaction:* African Greys are talkative when they desire attention and often seek out social interactions. Your parrot may be expressing a longing for company if it is crying out or whistling. Your relationship with your bird will become stronger and this habit will be reinforced if you interact with it and respond well to its cries.

Reading Nonverbal Cues

Birds use body language in addition to vocalizations to communicate. You can determine your African Grey's requirements and mood by observing its body language. The following typical body language indicators should be recognized:

- *Feather Position*: Your parrot's mental condition may be revealed by the way its feathers are arranged. Feathers that are puffed up might indicate that your bird is sick, scared, or cold. On the other hand, smooth feathers often signify that your parrot is at ease and content.

- *Head Bobbing:* An African Grey's common way of communicating is by bobbing their head. Head bobbing might be interpreted as a plea for attention, playful behavior, or enthusiasm. When your bird shakes its head, talk to it; this will improve your relationship.

- *Tail posture:* Your parrot's tail posture might also provide information about its emotional state. A depressed tail may imply pain or anxiety, whereas an erect tail usually denotes interest and eagerness. To get a better understanding of your bird's emotions, pay attention to its general posture and body language.

- **Beak Movements:** In addition to using their beaks for feeding, African Greys use them to explore their surroundings and communicate their feelings. A parrot that is nibbling or chewing on its toys softly is probably happy and interested, but an aggressive chewer or biter may be under stress or feel threatened.

Communication and Vocalizations

In addition to their remarkable capacity to imitate human speech and noises, African Grey

Parrots have a vast lexicon of vocalizations of their own that have many meanings. Gaining an awareness of these vocalizations can help you better comprehend the wants and feelings of your bird.

- *Calling and Whistling:* In order to attract their owners' attention, African Greyhounds often cry out or whistle. Usually pleasant, these vocalizations indicate your bird's desire for engagement. Positive responses to these calls will help to reinforce the behavior.

- *Screaming:* Shouting excessively may be a sign of attention-seeking, boredom, or irritation. Examine your African Grey's surroundings for indications of boredom or unfulfilled demands if it is screaming. Intense vocalizations may be lessened by offering social engagement and enrichment activities.

- ***Mimicking Sounds:*** African Greys are skilled mimics and may replicate noises they hear often, including doorbells, ringing phones, and even brief exchanges of speech. This behavior, which is often playful, shows that your parrot is interested in its surroundings.

- ***Chattering and Purring:*** Mild chattering or purring noises often indicate satisfaction and ease. If your bird is perched and producing these noises

It's encouraging that it feels safe and cozy near to you.

Recognizing Fear and Aggression

African Grey Parrots may be friendly and loving, but in certain situations, they can also show fear or violence. It is essential to comprehend the underlying reasons of these behaviors in order to manage and mitigate them.

Territorial Behavior: African Greys have a tendency to be possessive, particularly in the vicinity of their cage or preferred perches. It's important to respect your parrot's limits and provide it the security it needs if you see it acting aggressively when you approach it in its area. Territorial behavior may be decreased with the use of positive reward and gradual desensitization.

- ***Fear Responses:*** African Greys may have fear reactions in response to environmental changes, loud sounds, or strangers. Screaming, flailing wings, or trying to get away are some indications of panic. It's important to offer your parrot a secure and tranquil environment and to give it the freedom to flee if it shows signs of anxiety.

- *Stress and Anxiety:* Because birds are sensitive to environmental changes, stress may result in unfavorable behaviors. Look for possible stressors in your bird's environment and habits if you see symptoms of stress in them, such as excessive vocalization or plucking of feathers. Reduce anxiety by eliminating abrupt changes and implementing stable habits.

Establishing a Good Connection

Take into consideration the following tactics in order to foster a happy and healthy connection with your African Grey:

- *Consistent Interaction:* Give your parrot frequent, high-quality attention. Take part in bonding activities with your partner, such fun, training sessions, and tender caressing.

- *Positive Reinforcement:* To promote desired actions, use positive reinforcement strategies. When your parrot exhibits good behaviors, such vocalizing or peaceful interaction, show it your appreciation by giving it gifts, praise, or love.

- *Patience and Understanding:* It takes time and patience to form a friendship with an African Grey. Pay close attention to the indications and reactions from your bird, and modify your interactions according to its comfort level. By honoring your parrot's limits, you may build rapport and trust.

Final Thoughts

To provide African Grey patients the best treatment possible, it is important to comprehend their behavior and communication. You may establish a setting that satisfies your bird's emotional and psychological requirements by reading their body language, vocalizations, and social signals. A satisfying connection with your feathery friend may be achieved by patiently developing a deep link via regular engagement, positive reinforcement, and patience. A happy and healthy parrot, ready to display its amazing personality and intellect, is an African Grey parrot that is well-understood.

CHAPTER 13:

FREQUENTLY ASKED QUESTION AND ANSWERS (FAQS)

The following are 12 often asked questions (FAQs) about your book on keeping African Grey Parrots as pets, along with their responses:

What distinguishes African Grey Parrots as pets from other birds?

Reaction: African Grey Parrots are well known for their remarkable social skills, remarkable intellect, and capacity to imitate human speech. They are interesting companions since they develop close relationships with their owners and need mental and social stimulation.

FAQ 2: What is the lifespan of African Grey Parrots?

Reaction: When given the right care, African Grey Parrots may live for 40 to 60 years or more. Due of their lengthy longevity, prospective owners must be ready to dedicate a significant amount of time to their upkeep and welfare.

What should I feed my African Grey Parrot? is the third FAQ.

Reaction: High-quality pellets should make up the majority of an African Grey Parrot's healthy diet, which should also include fresh fruits and vegetables, seeds, and sometimes nuts. It is also essential to guarantee that they always have access to clean water.

FAQ 4: What is the best way to train an African Grey Parrot?

Reaction: Positive reinforcement methods, such as target and clicker training, may be used to teach African Grey Parrots. Training must be done with patience, consistency, and quick incentives for desired actions.

FAQ 5: What health problems are typical in African Grey Parrots?

Reaction: African Grey Parrot health problems include obesity, psittacosis, feather plucking, respiratory infections, and female egg-binding.

For the purpose of early identification and treatment, regular veterinarian checkups and observation for symptoms of sickness are essential.

FAQ 6: What symptoms might indicate a sick African Grey Parrot?

Reaction: Aside from physical abnormalities like swelling or feather loss, aberrant droppings, altered vocalization, hunger changes, and tiredness are also indicators of disease in African Grey Parrots. Seek quick veterinary advice if you see any troubling signs.

FAQ 7: Do African Grey Parrots need company or can they be maintained alone?

Reaction: Although they may be maintained alone, African Grey Parrots prefer company and socialization, whether it comes from other birds or their owners. Their wellbeing depends on receiving frequent mental stimulation and contact.

FAQ 8: What is the required amount of room for an African Grey Parrot?

Reaction: African Grey Parrots need a roomy cage with enough space for toys and perches so they may walk about comfortably. A bigger cage is usually preferable, and they should also have regular opportunity to explore outside their cage in a secure area.

FAQ 9: What type of toys for my African Grey Parrot should I get?

Reaction: African Grey Parrots need toys that provide both mental and physical stimulation. Provide a range of toys, including interactive ones that encourage play and discovery, puzzles, chewables, and foraging toys.

FAQ 10: Do African Grey Parrots make peaceful or noisy pets?

Reaction: African Grey Parrots are renowned for their loud cries and mimicry, and they may be rather talkative birds. They can be educated to be quieter, but in order to curb their excessive vocalization, they do need a lot of connection and mental stimulation.

FAQ 11: How often should I see the veterinarian with my African Grey Parrot?

Reaction: It is advised that you take your African Grey Parrot for a yearly examination by a veterinarian. However, you should contact a veterinarian right once if you see any symptoms of sickness or changes in behavior.

FAQ 12: How can I improve the surroundings of my African Grey Parrot?

Reaction: Give your African Grey a variety of toys, change them out often, and give foraging opportunities to make their habitat more enjoyable. Include engaging toys, climbing structures, and frequent socialization to keep your bird engaged both cognitively and physically.